Contents

How you think and feel   4

Your brain   6

Your nerves   8

Two sides of the brain   10

Learning   12

Your senses   14

Using words   16

Remembering   18

Being creative   20

Feeling happy or sad   22

Feeling afraid   24

Sleeping and dreaming   26

Looking after your brain   28

Glossary   30

Useful information   31

Index   32

How you think and feel

YOUR BRAIN lets you think and feel. When you were a baby, you cried when you felt hungry or thirsty and you smiled when you felt safe and happy. Your brain was controlling these feelings.

As you came to know more sights and sounds, your brain stored the memory of these things so you would recognize them again. You learned how different things felt, smelled or tasted. You learned to crawl and then to walk. You learned to understand words and to speak.

DID YOU KNOW?
There is no link between the size of your brain and cleverness. People with small brains can be as clever as those with bigger brains.

Babies start to smile when they are just a few weeks old.

4

The Body in Action

Thinking and Feeling

Jillian Powell

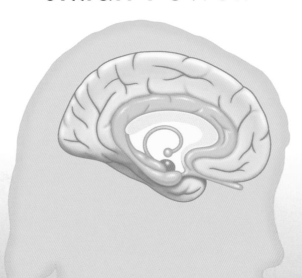

Titles in this series:
Eating
Moving
Seeing
Thinking and Feeling

Copyright © 2004 Bailey Publishing
Associates Ltd

Produced for A & C Black by
Bailey Publishing Associates Ltd
11a Woodlands
Hove BN3 6TJ

Editor: Alex Woolf
Designer: Stonecastle Graphics
Artwork: Michael Courtney
Cartoons: Peter Bull
Picture research and commissioned
photography: Ilumi Image Research
Consultant: Dr Kate Barnes

First published in 2004 by
A & C Black Publishers Ltd, 37 Soho Square,
London W1D 3QZ
www.acblack.com

British Library Cataloguing in Publication Data

ISBN 0 7136 63375

J170,985 E18

A & C Black uses paper produced with elemental
chlorine-free pulp, harvested from managed
sustainable forests.

Printed in Hong Kong
by Wing King Tong.

Picture Acknowledgements:
Corbis: Charles Gupton: 26; **Getty Images:**
Benelux Press: 24, Tim Brown: 29b, Bill
Hickley: 5b, Geoff Franklin: 18, Michael
Krasowitz: 16, Lester Lefkowitz: 29t, Elyse
Lewin: 4, Photomondo: 22, Mark Romanelli:
20, Frank Siteman: 10, Jacob Taposchaner: 28,
Arthur Tilley: 5t, 6, 8, Ross Whitaker: 12;
Pictor: Jeffrey Rich: 14.

Your brain controls the eye and hand skills that you need to play games. Practice improves these skills.

During the first five years of your life, your brain began to store **memories**, and you began to think for yourself. You knew what your favourite foods were, and what you liked to read or watch on television. You began to use your brain to work out sums, to understand how to play games and to plan things to do.

When you hit a ball your brain tells your body how and when to move.

5

Your brain

YOUR BRAIN is a large, spongy ball inside your head which looks like a giant walnut. It is soft and needs protecting, so there is a hard covering of bone all around it.

Your brain has three main parts. The largest part is the **cerebrum**. It is at the top of your brain and controls all your **senses**. In the middle is your **brain stem**. All the signals that pass between your brain and your body go through here. Behind the brain stem is another area called the **cerebellum** or 'little brain'. This part controls the way you move your body.

Together, these three parts of your brain control how your body works.

DID YOU KNOW?
An average adult human brain weighs 1.4 kilograms. An elephant's brain can weigh up to 6 kilograms. A cat's brain weighs in at 30 grams, and a rabbit's brain weighs even less at 10 grams.

Your brain is active even when you are asleep. It helps your body to grow and heal injuries. It also sorts through all the information you have taken in during the day.

This girl is using three different parts of her brain as she does a sum on a calculator.

The cerebrum is the largest part of the brain. It controls your thoughts and **emotions**. You use this part of the brain when you think about a sum.

The **skull** is a thick layer of bone that protects the brain.

The **cerebellum**, or 'little brain', controls your balance and co-ordinates your movements. You use this part of the brain to move your fingers when using a calculator.

The **cortex** is the outer layer of the **cerebrum**. It receives signals from the **senses** and sends orders to different parts of your body. When you look at the screen of a calculator, the cortex receives the signals from your eyes.

The **brain stem** controls basic functions such as your heartbeat and breathing.

The **spinal cord** is a bundle of **nerves**. It carries signals between your brain and your body.

Your nerves

YOUR BRAIN is connected to your body by **nerves**. You have billions of nerves all over your body in a network called the **nervous system**.

Your **spinal cord** is your body's main nerve. It runs down your backbone, or **spine**, from the lower part of your brain. Nerves branch off it and go all over your body.

Every second, your nerves carry millions of signals from your eyes, ears, nose, tongue and skin to your brain. They tell it what is going on in your body and all around you. Your brain then sends out signals telling your body what to do. Some actions, like eating or walking, you choose to do, but your brain also makes sure your body does other things all the time. It tells your heart to beat and your **lungs** to breathe – even when you sleep.

When you score a goal at basketball, your nervous system first sends signals to your brain about the position of the ball, your arm and the net. Your brain then sends signals to move the right muscles.

DID YOU KNOW?
Multiple sclerosis (MS) is a disease which affects nerve signals from the brain to the body. The signals get weaker, making it hard to move.

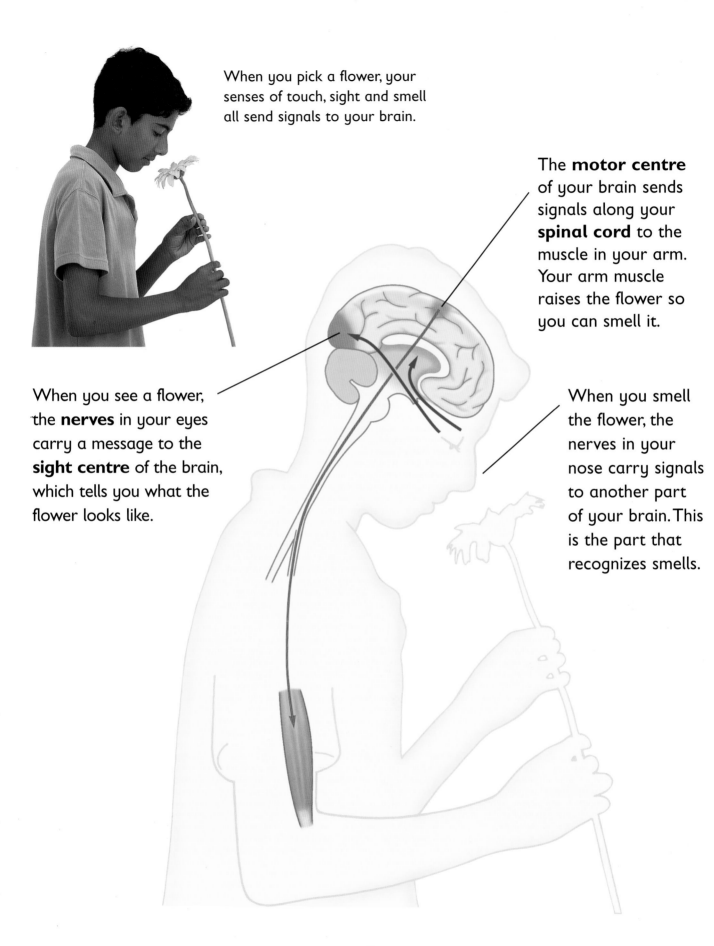

When you pick a flower, your senses of touch, sight and smell all send signals to your brain.

The **motor centre** of your brain sends signals along your **spinal cord** to the muscle in your arm. Your arm muscle raises the flower so you can smell it.

When you see a flower, the **nerves** in your eyes carry a message to the **sight centre** of the brain, which tells you what the flower looks like.

When you smell the flower, the nerves in your nose carry signals to another part of your brain. This is the part that recognizes smells.

Two sides of the brain

THE MAIN thinking part of your brain (the **cerebrum**) is divided into two halves. Each side controls the movements and **senses** on the opposite side of your body. So the right side of your brain controls the left side of your body, and the left side of your brain controls the right side of your body.

Each half of your brain is also in charge of particular skills. The left half of your brain controls skills such as speech and maths, while the right side controls creative skills such as art and music.

The two sides of your brain are connected by a bundle of **nerves** so they can exchange signals and information. For most activities you need both sides to work together. So, when you read the word *cat*, you use the left side of your brain to understand the word, and the right side to picture a cat in your mind.

The right side of the brain controls creative skills for most people.

Both sides of your brain work together to help you complete a jigsaw puzzle.

The right side of your brain helps you to imagine a jigsaw as a whole picture.

The left side of your brain helps you work out where the jigsaw pieces fit.

Nerves deep inside the brain join the right and left sides.

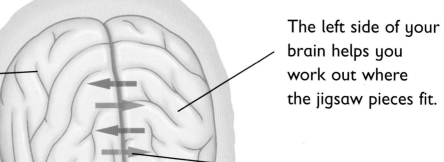

Learning

TO LEARN, your brain needs to take in lots of information from your **senses**, such as your eyes and ears. It sorts the information, storing the bits it needs and forgetting the rest. It then tells your body what it understands from the information, and what you need to do.

Your brain is made up of 100 billion tiny **brain cells**. When you think, nerve signals flash between these brain cells. They travel at around 350 kilometres an hour. Billions of signals can jump between your brain cells every second.

When you learn something new, the signals start to form patterns. As you practise your new skill, your brain recalls these patterns. Each time, the patterns become stronger and the task gets easier.

You learned to eat without having to think about it, but you need to practise other skills.

DID YOU KNOW?
Epilepsy is caused by brain cells firing off nerve signals faster than usual. When this happens the body shakes violently. This is called an epileptic fit and it lasts until the brain cells return to normal.

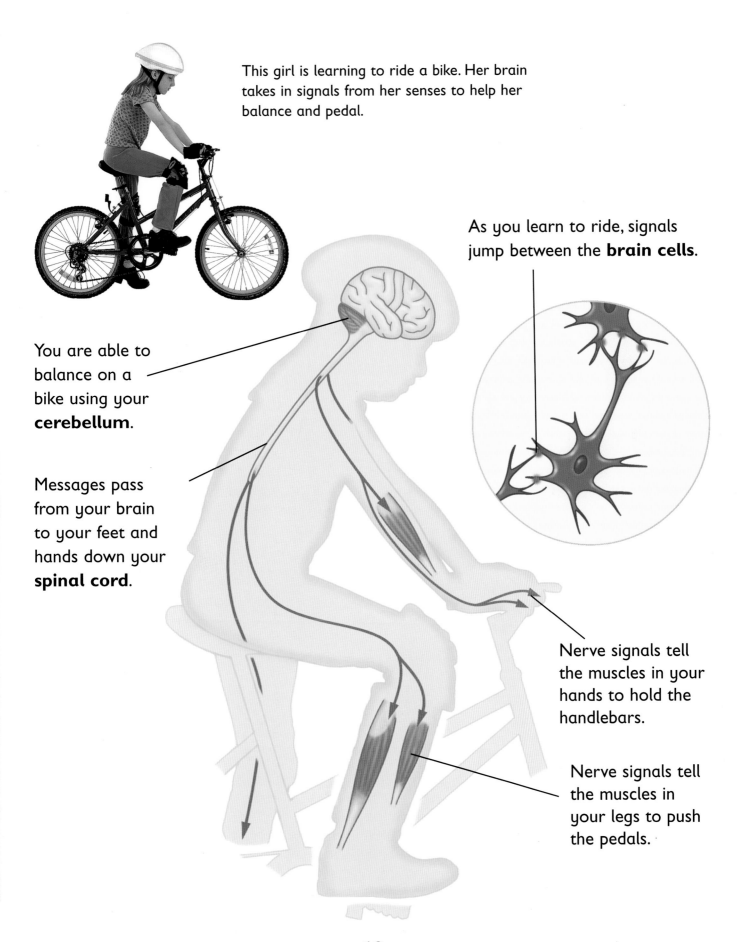

This girl is learning to ride a bike. Her brain takes in signals from her senses to help her balance and pedal.

As you learn to ride, signals jump between the **brain cells**.

You are able to balance on a bike using your **cerebellum**.

Messages pass from your brain to your feet and hands down your **spinal cord**.

Nerve signals tell the muscles in your hands to hold the handlebars.

Nerve signals tell the muscles in your legs to push the pedals.

13

Your senses

YOUR BODY has **receptors** in your skin which take in information from your five **senses** – sight, hearing, touch, smell and taste. The receptors turn the information into signals. **Nerves** carry these signals to your brain. Part of your inner brain sorts all the information from your senses.

A small part at the centre of your brain keeps a check on your body temperature and your appetite. If you feel too hot or too cold, it sends signals to make you sweat or shiver. If your body needs food or water, it sends signals that make you feel hungry or thirsty. Your brain also receives signals of pain when your body is hurt or unwell.

DID YOU KNOW?
Your brain keeps your body temperature the same, whether you are playing in the sun or snow. It makes chemicals in your blood that tell different parts of the body to warm up or cool down as needed.

When you feel cold, you shiver. This is because your brain tells your muscles to shake your body and warm you up.

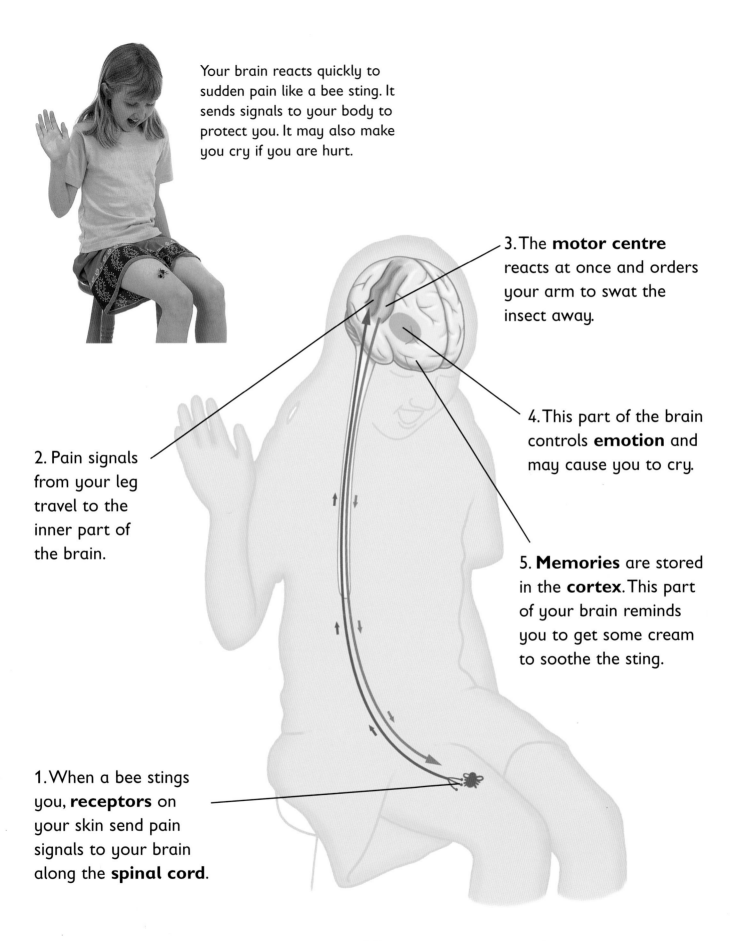

Your brain reacts quickly to sudden pain like a bee sting. It sends signals to your body to protect you. It may also make you cry if you are hurt.

3. The **motor centre** reacts at once and orders your arm to swat the insect away.

2. Pain signals from your leg travel to the inner part of the brain.

4. This part of the brain controls **emotion** and may cause you to cry.

5. **Memories** are stored in the **cortex**. This part of your brain reminds you to get some cream to soothe the sting.

1. When a bee stings you, **receptors** on your skin send pain signals to your brain along the **spinal cord**.

Using words

WHEN SOMEONE speaks to you, your ears pick up the sounds of the words and turn them into nerve signals which travel to your brain. Your brain then sends signals to the **speech centre** which works out what has been said.

To speak, your brain uses the speech centre to form words and sentences. It then sends signals to tell your **voice box**, throat, tongue and lips to make the sounds.

You also use your speech centre when you read. Your eyes take in the shape of letters and words and turn them into nerve signals. They send these signals to your brain so that it can work out the meaning of the words.

DID YOU KNOW?
Singing is good for you because it increases substances in your blood that fight germs!

When you write, signals move very quickly between your brain and your eyes and hand.

DID YOU KNOW?
People who have dyslexia find it hard to read, learn and write words because their brains muddle up letters and words. Dyslexia may be caused by problems in the way the brain sends signals to its speech centre.

When you read aloud you use many different parts of your brain.

2. The nerve signals travel from your eyes to the **sight centre**, which tells you what the words look like.

3. Signals are now sent from the **sight centre** to the **speech centre** of your brain. Here you make sense of the words.

1. First, your eyes take in the shapes of the words. They turn them into nerve signals.

4. Your brain sends signals to this area, where you work out how to say the words.

5. Finally, signals are sent to your **voice box**, throat, tongue and lips, which tell them to form the sounds of the words.

Remembering

YOUR BRAIN can store and recall ideas, events and even feelings in your **memory**. You have two types of memory: short-term and long-term. Your short-term memory stores events that have just happened. Your long-term memory stores experiences from your past.

Your long-term memory will never become full. By the time you are eight years old, it can store more information than a million encyclopaedias. It can go on storing new information all through your life.

Each time you form a new memory, one **brain cell** links up with thousands of others to form a pattern of signals that you can later recall.

When you are learning something, you use the same brain connections over and over again. You can recall patterns from your memory during a test.

DID YOU KNOW?
Your memory is like a muscle: it gets stronger every time you use it. If you do not use it, you will eventually forget things.

This girl is looking at old photographs. Her long-term memory helps her to remember things that happened years ago.

When you look at old photographs, you remember the feelings you had at the time in this area.

The **cortex** stores many **memories**, including exciting events.

Facts about the event are stored here, on the left side of the brain.

Emotional memories are stored in the centre of the brain.

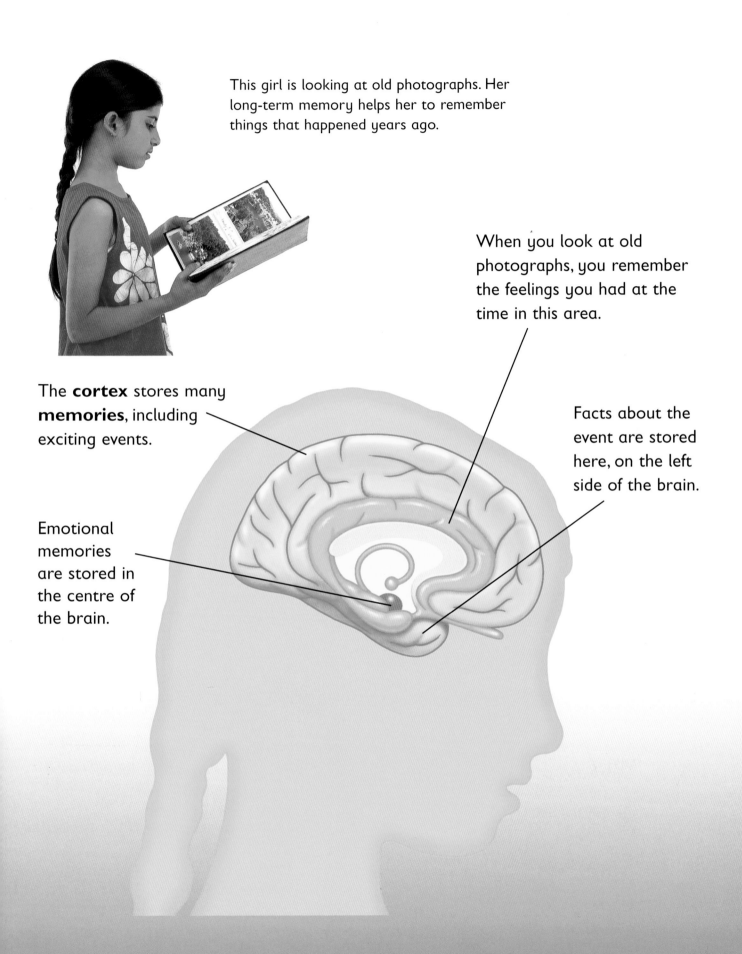

Being creative

YOU USE the right side of your brain when you are being creative. It helps you think about pictures or patterns. You use it when you are drawing or painting, playing a musical instrument, dancing, using your imagination or daydreaming. It also helps you recognize faces, shapes and patterns, and judge space and distance.

When you paint a picture, you use the thinking part of your brain to invent an idea. You may use **memories** stored in different parts of your brain. As you start to paint, your eyes send signals to the **sight centre** of the brain. Your hands send signals as you pick up and move the brush. Your brain sends signals back to the muscles in your arm and hands telling them what to do next.

DID YOU KNOW?
If you are right-handed, you can improve your creative skills by drawing with your left hand. This will exercise the right side of your brain.

DID YOU KNOW?
Your brain is unique. No two brains are shaped or wired exactly the same way, so we all have different skills and talents.

When you write a poem, you use different parts of your brain to find words to go with your feelings.

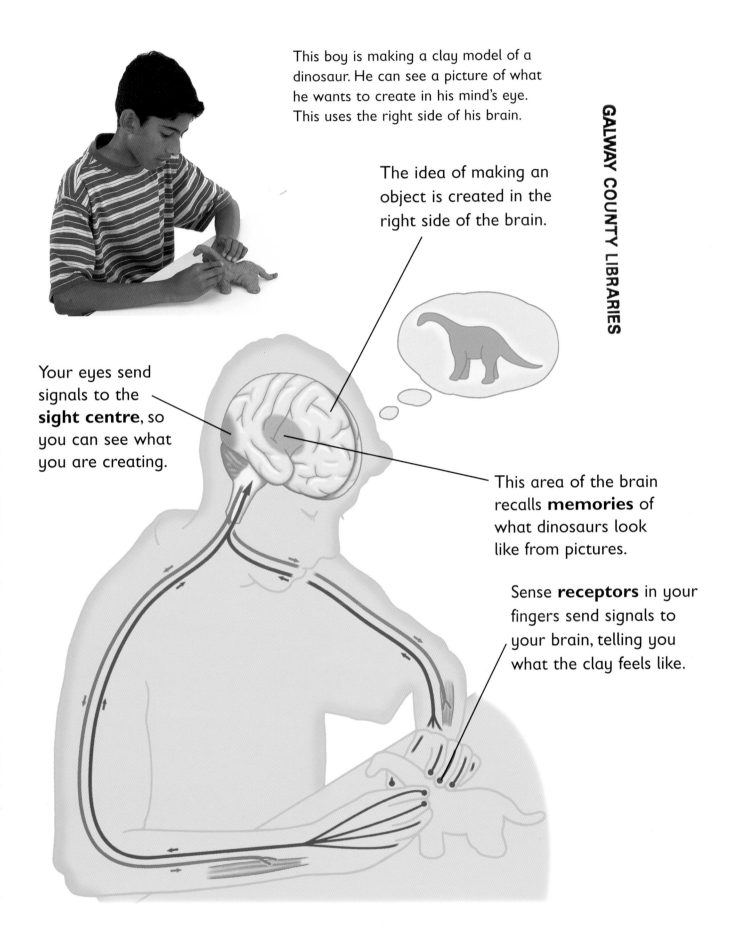

This boy is making a clay model of a dinosaur. He can see a picture of what he wants to create in his mind's eye. This uses the right side of his brain.

The idea of making an object is created in the right side of the brain.

Your eyes send signals to the **sight centre**, so you can see what you are creating.

This area of the brain recalls **memories** of what dinosaurs look like from pictures.

Sense **receptors** in your fingers send signals to your brain, telling you what the clay feels like.

Feeling happy or sad

WE ALL feel happy, sad or angry at different times. If you win a prize or a sports competition, you feel happy. If you have to say goodbye to friends, or if someone you love dies, you feel sad. We call these feelings **emotions**. They are controlled in a special area of your brain.

Your mood is changed by chemicals in your brain. A chemical called **serotonin**, for example, can give feelings of pleasure. The chemicals pass from one **brain cell** to another and carry signals between them. This affects how you feel.

DID YOU KNOW?

Chocolate contains chemicals that react with the chemicals in your brain to make you feel good!

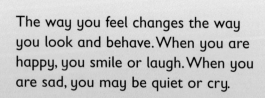

The way you feel changes the way you look and behave. When you are happy, you smile or laugh. When you are sad, you may be quiet or cry.

Scoring a goal activates chemicals in your brain and you experience a rush of excitement.

When you see the ball enter the net, nerve signals travel from your eyes to the **sight centre** of your brain.

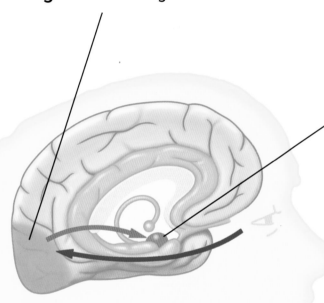

Your brain then sends signals to this area where you feel delight, and you shout for joy.

Feeling afraid

EVERYONE FEELS afraid or worried sometimes. Fear can make your heart beat faster and your mouth feel dry. You may even start to sweat. You sense fear in the same part of the brain that you sense happiness, sadness and other **emotions**.

When nerve signals tell your brain that you are feeling afraid, your brain prepares your body for escape. It sends out signals to slow down your **digestive system** so you can use energy for other things. It tells your heart to beat faster to pump more blood to your muscles, and tells your **lungs** to breathe faster to take in more air. Even the **pupils** in your eyes get larger so you can see well!

Your brain also tells your body to start making a **hormone**, or chemical, called **adrenalin**. Adrenalin puts your whole body on alert.

Adrenalin can help us in any situation where we feel pressure. It can even help us do well in sports, but the effects only last for a short time.

DID YOU KNOW?
Scientists call our reaction to fear "fight or flight". They think it began in times when our ancestors were in danger from wild animals. They either had to fight or escape.

When you see or hear something that scares you, your brain tells your body to react fast.

When you are frightened you sense fear in this part of your brain.

Your heart rate increases to pump blood faster to your brain and muscles.

The **pupils** in your eyes get larger to let in more light and improve your eyesight.

Your **lungs** breathe faster to take in more air.

Your body starts producing **adrenalin** which puts your body on red alert.

Sleeping and dreaming

YOU SPEND about a third of your life asleep. When you feel tired, your brain sends out signals that make you go to sleep. Your breathing and heartbeat slow down and your muscles relax.

During the night you experience light sleep and deep sleep. Your brain is most active during light sleep: your heartbeat gets faster, your muscles twitch and your eyes move rapidly under your eyelids. This is when you dream. Some scientists think dreams are your brain's way of sorting through experiences and **memories**.

DID YOU KNOW?
Children dream for fifty percent of the night, and adults dream for twenty percent. You only remember your last dream, although you may have many during the night.

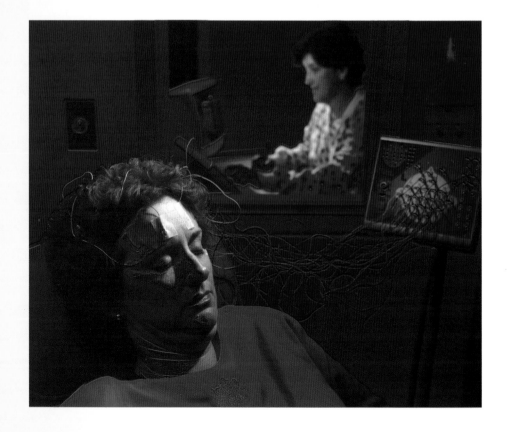

Scientists can watch a person's brain work during sleep. They use a special machine which records nerve signals in the brain as wavy lines on a computer screen.

Your brain and your body need sleep to keep them working properly. This is the time when your body grows and repairs injuries.

This is the sleep/wake centre in your brain. It sends messages to the rest of your brain to tell it when you need to sleep.

Your body sends signals that it is warm and comfortable along your **spinal cord.** They tell your brain you are ready to sleep.

While you are asleep, this part of the brain sorts information from the day and decides what to store and what to forget.

Looking after your brain

EXERCISE IS good for both your brain and your body because it boosts the part of your brain that helps you learn and remember. You can also exercise your brain by learning new things and doing brain-teasers, such as word and picture puzzles. Smoking and drugs can harm your brain, so you should always avoid them.

STAY HEALTHY

Eating lots of fresh fruit and vegetables keeps your body and your brain healthy. Strawberries and leafy green vegetables are especially good because they contain substances that protect your brain cells.

Safety gear protects your brain and body during active sports.

Doctors use scanning machines to look inside a patient's brain. From the pictures on the screen, they can see problems developing and decide what treatment a patient needs.

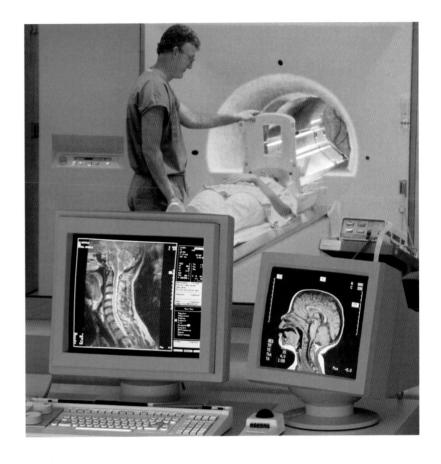

If someone damages one side of the brain, it affects the opposite side of the body. So if someone has a stroke in the left part of their brain, he may be unable to move the right side of his body. A stroke happens when a blood clot stops blood reaching part of the brain.

Glossary

adrenalin A hormone or chemical that your body produces when under pressure.

brain cell One of hundreds of billions of living units that together make up the brain.

brain stem The central core of the brain that is connected to the nerves in your spine.

cerebrum The largest part of the brain, which controls your senses.

cerebellum The part of the brain that controls co-ordination and balance.

cortex The outer layer of the brain.

digestive system The parts of the body that break food down so it is small enough to be absorbed.

emotions Strong feelings.

hormones Chemicals used to send signals around the body.

lungs Spongy organs that you use for breathing.

memory The ability to recall past actions and events.

motor centre The part of the brain that controls the body's movement.

nerve A long strand of special cells that sends signals round the body.

nervous system The system made up of the brain, spinal cord and nerves, which work together to let us touch, move and feel.

pupils The small, round opening at the front of the eye that lets in light.

receptor A nerve ending in the skin that can feel sensations such as warmth, cold and pain.

serotonin A chemical in your brain that affects your emotions.

senses The five senses are sight, hearing, taste, smell and touch. They give us information about the world around us and help to protect us.

sight centre The part of the brain that senses sight.

skull The bones that protect your brain.

speech centre The part of the brain that recognizes words and speech.

spinal cord A bundle of nerves that run down the spine.

spine The string of small bones running down the back.

voice box The part of your throat where sound is produced.

Useful information

Books

Your Body: Brain by Anna Sandeman (Franklin Watts, 2000)

Learning a Lesson by Steve Parker (Franklin Watts, 1991)

Your Amazing Brain (See-through View) Jenny Bryan (Wishing-Well Books, 1996)

CD roms

Become a Human Body Explorer (Dorling Kindersley, 2000)

Websites

www.soton.ac.uk
Neuroscience for kids with information, activities and experiments on the brain and nervous system.

www.kidshealth.org/kid/body/brain
Lots of information about the brain and body and how they work.

www.howstuffworks.com/brain.htm
Explains in simple terms how the brain works.

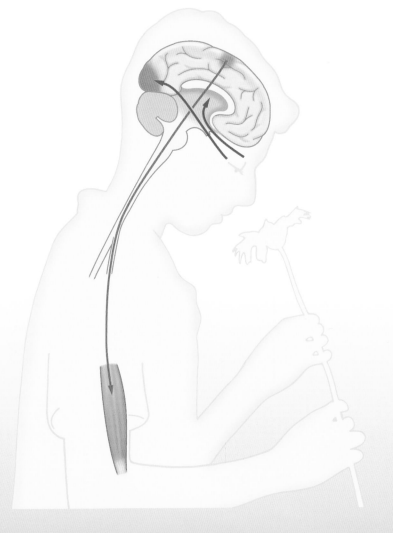

Index

adrenalin   24, 25, 30
animal brains   6
babies   4
balancing   6, 7, 13
brain
   brain stem   6, 7, 30
   cerebellum   6, 7, 13, 30
   cerebrum   6, 7, 10, 30
   cortex   7, 15, 19, 30
   motor centre   9, 15, 30
   sight centre   17, 20, 21, 23, 30
   sleep/wake centre   27
   speech centre   16, 17, 30
brain cells   12, 13, 18, 22, 28, 30
breathing   7, 24, 25, 26
creativity   20-21
digestive system   24, 30
dreaming   26-7
drugs   23, 28
dyslexia   16
eating   8, 12, 28
emotions   4, 7, 15, 18, 19, 22-5, 30
exercise   28
fear   24-5
feelings   (see emotions)
health problems
   epilepsy   12
   injuries   7, 27
   multiple sclerosis   8
   stroke   29
health and safety   28

heart   24, 25, 26
learning   4, 12-13, 28
maths skills   7, 10
memory   4, 5, 15, 18-19, 21, 26, 28
moving   6, 7, 8, 9, 10, 13
muscles   8, 9, 13, 14, 20, 24, 25, 26
nerves   8, 9, 10, 11, 13, 14, 30
nervous system   8, 30
pain   14, 15
painting   20
reading   10, 16, 17
receptors   14, 15, 21, 30
senses   4, 6, 7, 8, 9, 10, 12, 13, 14-15, 30
   hearing   12, 14, 16, 25
   seeing   7, 9, 12, 14, 16, 20, 23, 24, 25
   smelling   9, 14
   tasting   14
   touching   9, 14, 20, 21
serotonin   22, 30
skull   6, 7, 30
sleeping   6, 8, 26-7
speaking   4, 10, 16-17
spinal cord   7, 8, 9, 15, 27, 30
spine   8, 30
sports   5, 24, 28
temperature   14
thinking   4, 5, 7
vitamin B   8
writing   16, 20